Tell The Devil I've Changed My Mind

———————

WRITTEN BY

AMBASSADOR LYNN MORGAN

'If you are engaged for a battle for your life…' these are the words that introduced me to the elements of this message.

I call it a *message* rather than a book, because some people read books for entertainment or information. This book however, is here to deliver a **message**, a weapon to equip us on the power of "No!" when the devil says 'Yes'

There are many times in our lives when we don't seem to realize that we are being distracted by the enemy because it is done in such a palatable way, that we mistake it for the truth. This **message** seeks to equip you with the tools to determine 'lie' from 'truth':

… it brings you into understanding of who you are;

… it equips you with the tenacity to stand for God even against the ridicule of others;

… it equips you to discern whether your experiences are punishment or process;

…it equips you with 'faith understanding' and 'faith working' measures;

…it equips you for the fulfillment of your destiny in God;

… it equips you to be YOURSELF.

So when you have finished activating the knowledge gained from this **message** … the devil will understand he is on the wrong battlefield, because you have changed your mind about losing.

Pastor Felicia Johnson
Barbados

"I've just finished reading, "Tell the Devil, I've Changed My Mind". I feel as though my veil has been torn in two because it was such a personal, honest and raw account of your experiences. I am reminded of my own life. I feel vulnerable, exposed, yet hopeful and revenged. You have ripped the shade from the untruths of our misconceptions of self, planted by family, culture and religion."

Marsha Gay
Educator, Barbados

WOW! What an amazing book "Tell the Devil I've Changed My Mind"! I highly recommend this book to the young girl struggling with her image, to the man who needs to jump into purpose!! This book will put you back into the ring of life and cause you to CONTEND for the faith again!!! A must read!

Prophet Angelow Hickson
U.S.A

"Tell the Devil I've Changed My Mind". The title in itself speaks volumes of the book that you now hold in your hands and that I have had the distinct opportunity and privilege to read. Ambassador Lynn Morgan in this God inspired, empowering and life changing ministry tool, unearths the true roots of issues that plague the minds of those called by God but for whom "stinking thinking" has cumbered and restrained them from achieving their fullest potential; causing them to operate from Heaven to Earth rather than the reverse.

"As a man thinketh in his heart so is he", and Ambassador Lynn Morgan reveals, the heart of God and the heart you should carry towards the things of God, your purpose and life generally albeit exposing, defeating, defusing and destroying the enemy, the devil himself. She does this by letting you know how to change your mind, destroying the strong holds of the enemy and letting him know you have changed your mind!

This book is not just theoretical but experiential and is birthed out of a place of, "a life lived, lessons learned, practices set in perspective and the results seen". What you are about to do is embark on a journey to your fullness as you, "tell the devil you have changed your mind"!

Prophet-Teacher Sheldon R. Miller
Barbados

Publisher: Ambassador Lynn Morgan

#36 Stepney Plantation Tenantry, South District, St. George BB050400, Barbados

Cover, Design and Layout by Timothy Leach of NiCOMM Solutions, Barbados

ISBN 978-976-8265-44-9 (Paperback) International Copy

Tell the Devil, I've Changed My Mind!
Copyright © 2017 by **Lynn Morgan**

All rights reserved. No part of this book may be reproduced in part or in whole in any form or by any means without written permission from the author.

First Edition April 2017

Dedication

To my children, Tia-Lin, Jaheim and Tianna-Li. You are my seed in the earth and I pray that the truths in this book and the many that I have taught you will propel you into becoming all that God has ordained for you to be. May you walk in the freedom with which Christ has made you free!

Table of Contents

TELL THE DEVIL I'VE CHANGED MY MIND 1

FOREWORD 8

PREFACE 15

INTRODUCTION 18

CHAPTER ONE – STINKING THINKING 25

CHAPTER TWO – THE PAST 36

CHAPTER THREE – REJECTION 52

CHAPTER FOUR – FATHER 66

CHAPTER FIVE – FEAR 77

CHAPTER SIX – CALLED TO BE DIFFERENT 87

CHAPTER SEVEN – THE WORD 100

CHAPTER EIGHT – OVERCOMING ADVERSITY 124

CHAPTER NINE - EMBRACING THE NEW! 139

CHAPTER TEN – GUILT 152

CHAPTER ELEVEN- GIVE UP? NEVER! 161

CHAPTER TWELVE – MY TURNING POINT 175

CHAPTER THIRTEEN – THE CALL 186

APPENDIX 1 - SOME PRAYER POINTS 192

Foreword

If you're engaged right now in the battle for your life, get your armour ready because this book is a call to arms! You are being equipped to fight all the way through to the blissful, God directed, purposeful end. This is your time and you are destined to win.

Writer Lynn Morgan has used her life experiences, highs and lows, mountains and valleys to share with readers how to walk through the battle for your purpose and destiny. By recapping her life from childhood, her early relationship with her parents, life in school in Barbados, challenges with her body image and her evolution as a Christian among the saints, she has put into words the struggle of young people everywhere. In her story is the tale of failure and infallibility, trials and triumph, conformity and defiance that can easily resonate with so many of us. In the midst of telling this powerful life story, she's still living her purpose and she shares with clarity and confidence how she found her faith in God and the strength to fight for God's purpose in her life. You can find your purpose too and you can tell the Devil 'NO!'

This is the time to say to the enemy that he will NOT have your life. You WILL live and NOT die and you WILL live God's purpose for your life. Lynn has written a young Caribbean persons' manual for getting to live your 'best life.' If you thought that you were at the end of your rope and were about to give in to the viciousness of the battle raging around you, tell the Devil you've changed your mind and you are ready to fight.

From the first few pages to the world, Lynn masterfully shares the beauty of God's love for us in our imperfection by sharing personal and transformational experiences. She hasn't held back and by sharing so much of herself, she is perfectly poised to empower whomever reads this book. It's not an easy journey on this road called life, and Lynn tells us in vivid form just how challenging life has been for her and she reminds readers that they are not alone. You are not alone in your battle! There are those who have battled the same demons and many others yet they are not just still standing, they are living their best life for having fought and won!

By challenging our way of thinking and reasoning, Lynn brings the internal battle young people wage in their minds into the forefront of our consciousness.

She challenges readers to rethink the very mind-set that is holding them back. If you are going to fight, this book tells you to start by thinking differently because it begins with you. In the telling of her story through this book Lynn has had many 'Paul on the road to Damascus' experiences which have changed her life. This book is going to be one of yours.

After she has dealt with how you see yourself, she then moves on to explore in her very easy, personable way how those around you now deserve your attention. One of the most powerful things she declares is that you have to avoid absorbing what others have spoken over your life and declared over you. The things you have heard are not always right. They can be wrong! What happens if you believe what the Devil has used them to speak over you? You cannot win the battle

against yourself only to have those around you who don't know your purpose cloud your new found sense of clarity. All of those things that you have struggled with from a child which have shaped you into the person you are now are ancestral bonds and you CAN break them! This book urges you to face the battle frontally by starting with how you see yourself and then defining who you are in God's Kingdom by using your newly released spirit of discernment.

So in many ways this book is about you. Yes you! You've been battling yourself and the Devil is laughing. That is NOT God's purpose for your life and this book shows you how to get out of that rut.

Ambassador of the New, Lynn is issuing a clarion call to all believers to arm ourselves with a change in mind-set, the word of God, a commitment to change and to the emergence of the new you!

Sharp, insightful and beautifully written, this book is deeply compelling and is an excellent resource to equip God's people with the tools, weapons and tactical and strategic techniques needed to face life's battles. It is a wonderful tool for parents, guardians and teachers that shows the impact they have on young people around them. The enemy can use even those who know and love us to derail us from the path that God intended and we have an opportunity with this book to share with them just how impactful they can be - with the love of God or the vitriol of the Devil.

By the time you have come to the end of this book you should be on your knees. You should have changed your mind and told the Devil that you have a new plan. You should be basking in the comfort of God's love even as the battles continue to rage, confident that you will emerge victorious. You will be preparing for the emergence of your best self!

Preface

I am writing this book as a bellow, a shout into the earth that lets the world know that I Lynn Morgan am alive, well, and ready to be the expression of God's best. For a long time I lived a defeated, scared and mediocre life. One that was not lived from heaven to earth, but from earth to heaven. This finally changed when I realized who I am in the earth and exactly whom God has created me to be. It is important that we come to this realization if we are ever going to change the way we live our lives. In this book, I share snippets of some of my childhood and teenaged experiences in order to

demonstrate how the enemy will use whom we **think** we are to keep us in bondage and ultimately cause us to miss out on living God's truth about who we really are. My story is a reminder that the enemy's plotting and scheming against us is not relegated just to the moment we become Christians, it begins long before then with negative experiences from as early as birth, throughout childhood, adolescence and well into adulthood. These experiences shape our thinking and subsequently find expression in our belief system and the decisions that we make daily. It is my hope that by sharing *'my redemption song'*, many lives will be impacted and you the reader will feel emboldened to make the radical life changes that are necessary in order to follow God's blue print for your own life. This story is my own to tell, you will have your own. God is infinitely interested and invested in the success of both. In order to make the necessary changes to our thinking, He has provided the Holy Spirit as a helper to make the outcome, His will, plan and purpose, possible. The wife, prophetic psalmist, songwriter, author, teacher, mother, minister and woman that I am today is proof of this.

Ambassador Lynn Morgan
St. George, Barbados

INTRODUCTION

"When you've changed your mind, you can change your life!"

"Tell the devil, I've changed my mind!" What about you? What have you decided? Have you had enough of living life the way you've been doing it for the past couple of years? Or, should I ask, are you tired of NOT living?

I believe strongly that you're reading this book because like me, you have simply had enough. Something deep within your spirit tells you that you are not living your best life. It causes you to yearn for more, for, if this is all there is to life then something is definitely wrong. So, you have come to a crossroad. Good. That, my friend, is a very important part of this process of change. In order for there to be a new beginning, something in our lives and our way of thinking must come to an end.

The rescue mission for my thinking, as I like to call it, turned out to be one of the most significant decisions I have made in my life to date. When I re-examined my life and realized that many of my experiences could have gone much differently if I had a different type of pattern to my thinking, it challenged me to make some changes. I discovered that when negative emotions such as fear and doubt are common to our

way of thinking, they will always have a negative impact on our decision-making.

Decision-making is a part of our lives that none of us can escape. Even the act of making no decision is in itself a decision. The reality is that who we are and our quality of life is a direct result of the decisions that we make each day. Maybe like me, by the time you are finished reading this book you will agree that *stinking thinking* is the easy part but changing our thought patterns that's the process that requires the most work. Thankfully, we do not have to do this alone. If you are a believer in Christ, then you will have some help during this process, at least, that has been largely my

experience. If you are not a believer, the process is simple, just pause now, confess your sins and ask God to become your Father and Saviour. Yes, it is that simple. Now you have the Holy Spirit as your helper too.

*N*egative experiences create a mirage in our lives that can cause us to deviate from the path on which Christ intends for us to walk. This is where the enemy of our souls longs for us to dwell. He wants us to be stuck in our emotions, in our thinking and in our desires. He wants us to believe that we are just stuck. Why? Well it is simple really, if we are stuck, we will be distracted so that we are unable to see God's best and we will

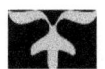

not believe that the Father has our best interests at heart. Neither will we aim to achieve His best for us.

My prayer is that the truth about what the Father wants to do in all of our lives will be clearly expressed across these pages as the story of *'my redemption song'* inspires you and ignites you to boldly follow the path that God has created for you to walk on. This is not just another self-help book, it is a charge to those who are walking in obscurity, not just because they are hidden but because of their belief systems. Many persons live insufferably below the level of God's best because they are still cocooned by the past and locked into an alternate reality foisted upon them by the circumstances of where they were born, whom they were born to, and the negative things that they have experienced.

As one who has survived what should have broken me, I live to declare the works of the Lord. My life is an expression of the fact that I have indeed changed my mind and I am now living God's best for me. Please do not get caught up in the word 'best' and expect that I am only referring to money, wealth, prosperity or riches. God's best is deeper than these material things. It means living out God's original intent for you with a boldness and confidence that defies the naysayers and confuses the enemy. It's when

we have tapped into that eternal spring of beauty, creativity and love that God has for each of us. Access to this place is available to us all.

CHAPTER ONE – STINKING THINKING

"The most dangerous lies we will ever tell are the ones we tell ourselves!"

One of the main reasons why we fail to achieve all that we can in our lives is because of the way we think. Pause. Now read that again.

I have found that this truth is so *simple* that we can literally gloss over it in our search for deeper meaning to answers about issues in our lives. In fact, I advance to you that wrong or poor thinking, what I have dubbed as *'stinking thinking'* is really

a trap that the enemy will use to imprison us and cause us to lack direction in our daily lives. Many life lessons have taught me that in order for anyone with this kind of thinking to **(ever) achieve anything positive or great in life**, they must *first* change their way of thinking.

I do not know what your experience has been, but it took longer for me to come to this realization than I really want to admit. I had to go through some disappointments, many disappointments really, bad decisions, self-doubt, fear, hurt and even despair before I recognized that the root of my problem was embedded in the seat of my *'stinking thinking'*. It was official. I

either had to change my thinking or continue to merely exist. There was no question for me really because undoubtedly, I wanted to LIVE!

The quality of life we live is intricately tied to our way of thinking. We can serve God, love Him with all of our hearts, mind and soul; we can worship Him sincerely, serve others faithfully, be actively involved in various ministries and still not LIVE! I believe that this is why Jesus said that He came so that we might have life and life more abundantly. One of the saddest things in life is to live with regret and to leave this earth without ever having lived! Living comes down to the very choices that we make in our

daily lives. Either we must decide to be exactly who God wants us to be and trust me this type of living depends heavily on the way we think; **or** we will become the expectations of others.

Fighting against the status quo is perhaps the one of greatest battles that we face in life. Popular culture is such a strong pull in our lives that many of us, instead of seeking to be exactly who God says we should be, are just content to make it through life by conforming to the norm. Sometimes we even settle for just *making a living*, instead of actually living.

Until we come to a place in our lives where we are confident in who we are and what we are about, we will define ourselves by the needs and motives of others. The irony of being caught in this web of other people's plans and other people's expectations is that some of these persons have absolutely no idea who we really are or what we can really do. But, because they have set themselves up as experts or because they are authority figures, we give them more say in our lives than we really ought to. Furthermore, in addition to not knowing who we really are, some persons are not even genuinely interested in our overall well-being, they are really just focused on themselves and their own needs. However, because they manage to pull us into their

space and drama, we mistake being needed for something it is not. Then, when we are sucked in and totally gullible, we miss the mark because our *stinking thinking* leads us to make poor choices. Sadly, my friend, since many of the choices we make are cleverly disguised as the popular choice we feel that we are choosing wisely. In other words, everybody else is doing it or this is the way it is has always been done either in our society or in our family structures.

In the Caribbean, and I believe that this is largely due in part to our heritage from slavery, we are taught <u>not</u> to question authority and <u>not</u> to give '*back chat*'.[1] We are instructed in this way both at home by our parents and other family members and it is reinforced at school by our teachers and principals. It is a common thing for children to be told to '*hush up*'.[2] This stems out of the belief that children should be seen and not heard. Other institutions in our society like the church and other clubs then perpetuate this stance. Now by no means am I recommending rebellion, although I have been accused of this on more than one occasion. No, in its stead I am suggesting

---

[1] Back chat – to be cheeky in your response to someone who is in authority. In the Caribbean we are taught that authority figures such as parents, teachers, pastors and other leaders always have the final say and to question their authority is frowned upon.

[2] To 'hush up' is a Bajanism which means to be quiet.

that sometimes, many times, we need to go against this status quo and ask questions. We need to fight the fear of being different and of being rejected and ask questions of people and of situations. Probe further; go beyond what is at face value to find out 'why' for ourselves. Better yet, we should be a people who are never afraid to ask God first and then listen to what He has to say. This would save many of us from much of the heartache that we face in our lives. I know for sure it would have saved me!

The battle is on for the fulfilment of our purpose and destiny in the earth. We are not exactly who God says we are to be because we battle with low self-esteem, a poor self-image or concept and erroneous thinking in spite of what God says about us in His word. Many of us experience feelings of hopelessness as we ask ourselves: How do I rise above my circumstances? How do I arise when the situations that I am facing seem to be continually holding me back? How do I keep going in the face of so many adversities? When will I reach the point where like the Apostle Paul I can say, "I've finished my course?" How can I accomplish positive things when all that I see when I look around is negative? Is it possible for me to arise when I am continually caught in a web and cycle of sin?

We often read the words *"With God all things are possible"*, or *"I can do all things through Christ who strengthens me"*. We may even repeat these words as a mantra, yet to our dismay we do not really see things changing in our lives. They just do not seem to be working. You may find yourself asking, "Where is God in all of this? How can I achieve all that God says I can?" This book is a part of my testimony of how my life transformed when I changed my *stinking thinking*. My life's journey so far has been fraught with difficulties, disappointments, challenges and even failures. However, I believe that the principles and experiences I openly share here will help you in your personal journeys as you delve deeper into your relationship with the Father and seek to move to a place of fulfilling your purpose and destiny, from a place of obscurity into a place of flourishing greatness. Trust me it's all tied up in how determined and committed you are to the process of changing your *'stinking thinking'*.

CHAPTER TWO – THE PAST

"What if who you are today is based on the lies the devil told you through your childhood experiences?"

"Can't they tell that I'm too smart for this class? What's wrong with my teachers? I know that I can read better than all of these children in here! I'm smart dammit, and there's no way I'm staying in this class one more day!"

This is one of the few very vivid memories that I still have of my childhood. God has used it to show me exactly who I am – the real me, who I was, before the devil tried to defeat and destroy me. After making the decision to leave my class, I did it every day. I daily left my assigned class to sit in another class (same age group, more advanced) where I perceived in my little mind that the children were smarter or as we would say in Barbados, 'brighter' than the ones in my assigned class. I boldly repeated this action every day in spite of the constant scoldings and 'lashes'[3] foisted upon me by irate teachers who only saw my 'rebellion' but did not understand the motive for my decision. Yet, I persisted every single day until one day my teachers came together and said, *"You know what, this child is brilliant! We simply cannot hold her back by keeping her in this*

---

[3] Lashes from the teacher were commonplace at this time as there was no law against the use of corporal punishment in schools.

class, she really belongs in that other class." You see, they had finally come to the same realization that I had already been convinced of for a while. This scenario alone could set the scene for me to tell you how sometimes in life we have to persist in what we believe in and are convinced of about ourselves irrespective of what others around us may think. An important lesson I have learned in life is that we cannot allow others people's opinions of us to become our reality. Instead, our reality must emanate directly out of the truth that God has spoken to us and over us. His truth alone must create our reality. But I am jumping ahead of myself a bit here.

It was the first term of the school year and I was six years old and assigned to Infants A2 when I first decided that the class to which I was assigned was really beneath my true level of ability and became determined that if my teachers did not recognize my true abilities, then I would have to show them. By the second term of this same school year, I got the victory that I had held out for when my teachers reassigned me to Infants A1, the class to which I knew deep down in my little convinced heart was where I truly belonged. As a part of this class, I excelled beyond my teachers' imagination. By the end of that school year's assessments, I received perfect

scores (100%) in all except one subject. I scored 95% in that one. I was brilliant, confident and persistent and I had proven it. *I knew who I was and no-one could tell me differently because somewhere deep down in my 'knower' I was convinced, confident and determined to show them exactly who I was.* This was the attitude of a winner. This was the attitude of someone who could achieve anything they put their mind to. This girl would grow up to be type of woman who would laugh in the face of adversity, who would continue on the path that she was convinced of no matter who or what stood in her way. This is how God had determined I should live even before the very foundations of this world.

I wish I could assure you that this self-assured child continued on this same path throughout her life and that an equally confident adult eventually emerged. If that were indeed the truth, there would be absolutely no need for this book. Alas, the things I experienced almost convinced me that I was really the exact opposite of who God said I was. Unfortunately - *fortunately in retrospect* - due to a number of situations in my life I was forced to take the scenic path enroute to becoming who I am today.

Whilst there are somethings about my life and circumstances that I would change

today if I could, the one constant in my life would be my parents. They are both deceased today but the role that they played in my life was paramount to the process that shaped me into who I am today. Although I love and miss them both dearly, I had to come to the point where I realized that God's plan, purpose and timing are more important than any other plans that we could possibly craft for ourselves. Oftentimes they far outweigh the plans that even our own parents have for us.

After joining this new class, I continued to excel and baffle my teachers for a few more years. I finished primary school as one of the top students and went on to one of the oldest and best secondary schools in our island. The reality was that I should have been the top student not just *one of* the top students. The Father has gifted me with a photographic memory and the ability to grasp concepts easily, I spoke and wrote extremely well by the time I was eleven years old. In fact, at that age, I can distinctly remember teaching students in my neighbourhood how to spell and complete their English assignments; and they were already attending secondary school! However, in spite of these innate abilities, life had beat me down so much that I had lost my shine. I was no longer that persistent, confident, somewhat arrogant child who

stood up for herself no matter who tried to hold her back. I was a mere shell of my former self. You see I had been subject to continuous emotional abuse at the hands of both my mother and father. Due to this treatment, I no longer believed that I was special and that I had the ability to achieve anything that I put my mind to. Because of the constant negative words that I received, I believed them and I settled for something even worse than failing. I settled for the belief that I was average, just an ordinary girl, no-one special, no-one important, no real purpose except to go to school and get a good job so that one day I could get out of my parent's home.

Let me first emphatically state that I have absolutely no malice towards my parents. At the time each passed away, we had had a healed relationship. One where I outwardly and vocally expressed my love and appreciation for them and they for me. What I will share about them is not intended to tarnish these two beautiful souls rather it is to expose the **rot** of the enemy and his plans to kill, steal and destroy our purpose and destiny in life. He is the real reason behind the negative experiences that we have. Our real fight is not with flesh and blood, so although my parents' actions affected me I know that they were just *tools* used by the enemy. Our real fight is against

the powers of darkness and spiritual wickedness in high places (Ephesians 6 vs. 12). His intention is to ensure that generation after generation continues to be separated from God. But, alas, God has other plans for us, plans to prosper us and to give us hope and a future (Jeremiah 29 vs.11). Furthermore, when our father and mother have forsaken us He is the one who takes us up. In my case, they have not forsaken me but they are deceased. Their deaths did not create the orphan that the enemy hoped for, rather, it opened me up to experience the love and comfort of God, who is and has become my **Real Father**.

My life's experiences have caused me to discover that we can grow up with parents who have absolutely no idea who we are, or the type of destiny that lies within and ahead of us. My parents did the best they could with what they had but the reality is that what they had was based on their own experiences and circumstances.

Growing up, just as any child should, I thought that they were my whole world, nothing abnormal about that, or so I thought. My experiences since their deaths have caused me to recalibrate my thinking. My parents were in fact, only a small part of my life. It is customary for us to fashion our lives after the experiences we have when we

were growing up and to see our future through the myopic lenses of the expectations of our parents and immediate family. We inherit a worldview based on the experiences of our parents and the worldview that they have inherited and adopted based on their own experiences. Sometimes there is absolutely nothing wrong with that, at other times this worldview is too simplistic or myopic for the vision that God has for us and our lives. In essence, sometimes our inherited worldview bids us to be contained whereas, God does not want us to be contained, He really wants us to grow and expand our territory. The vision He has for us far outweighs our parent's plans and what we ourselves could even think or imagine.

When I speak of containment, I speak both literally and figuratively. Sometimes we are not only bound by the confines of the thinking or worldview created for us, sometimes it's literal, and we are geographically bound. We remain in the same neighbourhood, with the same neighbours as our parents. We stay in the same church for many years refusing to broaden our horizon by new experiences.

The experience of Jabez found in 1 Chronicles chapter four (4) clearly illustrates what I am speaking about. Jabez's mother experienced great pain whilst she was in

labour with him. Because of this, she gave him a name based solely on her circumstances and her reality. She named him Jabez, which meant that he was conceived in great pain. Jabez's mother was unable to look ahead at who her son would become. Instead, she created a reality for him based solely on her experiences and worldview at the time. It was the same for my parents, they raised me based on their own childhood experiences and worldview. They were unable to think of what my future should look like because the realist thing for them was the reality of their experiences and the circumstances into which I was born.

This type of childhood experience is the kind of deception that the enemy uses to keep many of us in bondage. When we buy into this type of thinking, we become so bound that we often never try to change our circumstances too dramatically. We instead just settle for what we determine to be our norm. We become stuck in the status quo and in the belief that this is who we were born to be. We accept that this is the way it was done by everyone in our family, or as we say in Barbados, *'my navel string buried right here'*, so we determine this is where we live and this is where we will stay for the rest of our lives. Thankfully, these experiences do not have to have the final say in our lives. Like Jabez, we too can take action to change our lives.

CHAPTER THREE – REJECTION

"You can be rejected by man but totally accepted by God!"

"You're a slut!" "You are a whore." "You're only interested in men and nothing else." "You're so lazy!" "You're not going to grow up to achieve anything in life."

These are just some of the negative words spoken to me by my mom whilst growing up. More often than not, a slap across the face accompanied these words. I don't know if you have ever experienced being slapped in the face, but let me tell you, it is one of the most degrading feelings you will ever experience. A slap in the face makes you feel really insignificant and unimportant. The shame and embarrassment fiercely belittles you. These slaps would wound me very deeply. They hurt to the very core of my being. Each time I received one, I imbibed a deeper message that I was no one important. My younger sister was never subject to this type of treatment. This further convinced me that I was getting just what I deserved. The slaps hurt more than the words that she spoke and those words cut me to my core, they dissected my soul.

In retrospect, now that I too am a mother, I have deduced that when my mum uttered these words they were really just an

expression of her inner fear that I would not turn out the way she hoped but to the younger me these words were like arrows to my soul. The constant piercings of these arrows produced a sadness and dejection that were far reaching when combined with my other negative experiences. Fortunately, due to this crazy innate strength and determination that were given to me by God, I was able to fight against becoming the words that were spoken over me but it was a long, uphill battle fraught with tears and bitterness. I could never understand why I was not loved the way I was supposed to be loved or rather the way I expected to be loved. I felt rejected and less than those around me, especially my younger sister who without effort, seemed to earn all the love, respect and acceptance that I longed for from my mother. The words my mum used and the way she expressed her *'fear'* sorry *'love'* were my kryptonite.

In addition to being determined and confident, I was also very soft spoken, sensitive and expressive. Some of these character traits were innate, others were created by the negative circumstances I faced around me. I was constantly made to feel like I was weak because I cried easily and hurt deeply when others spoke to me. *"You're wicked, that's why you cry so easily."* These are the words I would hear when after

being punished I would cry incessantly for the day and sometimes days ahead. In reality, I was just broken, so broken that each time a new wound was inflicted I would sink further and further into the depressive rut that was my life.

It is important to understand though that this same sensitivity is what God uses to help me to empathize with others who are facing similar conditions or situations that cause pain. My sensitivity was an undeveloped gift from the Father that the devil was using my parents, especially my mum to tarnish and to cause it to appear to be something ugly that I should grow up to reject about myself. Today, this sensitivity

enables me to feel the pain of others that I minister to and leads me to pray specifically for their healing. It causes me to walk alongside other broken souls who are in need of repair and offer solace and a place of healing that is free of judgement. My main point here is to emphasize that although my sensitivity was a gift from God, it was tainted in my eyes for many years. My parents' treatment was another negative childhood experience that sought to thwart a ministry that God had placed deep on the inside of this formerly broken child. What about you my friend? What gifts has God placed deep on the inside of you that the

enemy has tried to belittle or downplay in your own life?

For a while I imbibed the negativity that was espoused almost daily by my mum. It seeped into my soul and crippled me in most areas of my life. I no longer tried to be the best at anything because in my little mind it did not make sense. Mediocrity became my friend and it appeared that the enemy's plan was working.

"Ha, ha, ha, ha!" "Look at her!" they pointed and shouted. "Look at those chubby legs go." "Oh my goodness, is she running backwards?" laughed another?"

"Has she stopped?" inquired one lady.

"Ha, ha, ha, ha!" they laughed and jeered.

It was me they were laughing so hard and pointing at. I was the object of their bemusement and ridicule. I was five years old and very excited about running in the children's race at church sports. After seeing all the other races before I could not wait to win my race. Thoughts of failure never even crossed my mind. Like anything else I attempted at this time of my life it was just another challenge that I could counter. Something happened when I started the race though. I ran with all my might but for the life of me I just could not keep up with the other kids. I started out strongly with the others but before I could even get halfway down the track I started to huff and puff and

run out of wind, I got tired and slowed almost to a halt. Instead of encouraging me to go on though, these adults and children saw absolutely nothing wrong with laughing, pointing and ridiculing me. I can still remember with great clarity the feelings of embarrassment and shame that washed over me. I knew something was not normal about me and they had all pointed it out. I was fat. I was overweight for my age and these people all saw it. I decided that day that I would never give these people or anybody else for that matter, the opportunity to laugh at me again. This was the day that I made one of the worst life decisions I could have ever made. A decision

I would pay dearly for later in life. I decided that physical activity was not for me because I was too fat to do it. I would never run in a race again, especially not at this church. This childhood experience scarred me and the fallout from this experience was tremendously far reaching.

I was only five years old and I was overweight. At this age, no child can be held responsible for his or her own health or wellbeing. Children at this age do not possess the understanding of how their body works. Neither do they have the responsibility for knowing the importance of a balanced diet and regular exercise. This is a result of their environment and familial

standards. It was only at this church event that I discovered that something was wrong with being fat, but fat I was, with no idea about how to change or control this fact. As long as I knew myself, that is who I was. My dad was fat, my mum was 'big boned'[4] and most of my sisters were overweight, except for my sister from my mother, the one who had her heart. Thus, this was a 'truth' that I accepted as my lot in life. Some people were slim, others were fat and there was nothing that could be done about it.

Stinking thinking will often cause us to settle. Thinking that has its base in these

---

[4] Big-boned – a term commonly used in the Caribbean to refer to persons who are fat or overweight but carry it well. They usually have tight skin as opposed to loose rolls of fat.

types of negative childhood experiences often results in *stinking thinking* and *stinking thinking* will cripple us and cause us to accept a reality that is flawed. It will cause us to believe things about ourselves that God has not spoken about us. My view of myself became tarnished and wrong thinking became a norm because of it. *What if the reality that you lived today is based on wrong thinking (stinking thinking) that you have, based on your childhood experiences?*

The good news is that as painful as our lives maybe, there is always a purpose to our pain and the things that we go through in our lives. Although abandoning the plan of God is sometimes the most tempting

alternative when we are faced with the difficulties and challenges of our circumstances, it is never the right solution. There are a few instances in the Bible, which indicate that these experiences are not unique to us. Some of the most significant people of God experienced abject rejection from people around them, including their families. Joseph was rejected by his brothers and sold into slavery because of his dream. Yes, he was his earthly father's favourite but that fact had absolutely nothing to do with his destiny. When Samuel was about to choose a king for Israel, David was neither his brothers' nor his father's choice for the position. Thus, he remained *hidden* until

God told Samuel that He does not look at the outward appearance like man, rather, He looks at the heart. In this scenario, it is interesting to note that not even the prophet, the man of God had any idea who God's chosen one was! (That's another book all by itself!). The principle is clear though, you can be born and raised into a family who has absolutely no idea who you are! Sometimes, even the prophet or man of God has no idea. If you really want to know who you are destined to be, you had better develop a personal relationship with the Father!

CHAPTER FOUR – FATHER
"A Father's Blessing?"

"Who do you look like though?" My dad pondered loudly one day. "You're not like your sisters, not really like your mum." "You're big, fat and black!" he declared.

Perhaps though, on reflection, the most defining words for me did not emanate from my mum, instead they erupted from the bowels of my dad. My father, whom I loved dearly with all my heart and whom I looked to as the one who really 'loved' me because he did not lash me like my mum did, neither did he say some of the things that she would, had actually uttered these word. Can you really fathom the pit that I sank into when my father cursed me with these words? For me, my father was the centre of my universe. He loved me! In fact, I had even played around with the idea that since my sister was my mom's favourite, I was his. It tore me up to find out in my teenaged years that his real synopsis of me was not that I was intelligent, beautiful or precious as I imagined he felt. No, he did not see anything of value when he looked at me. He did not assure me that one day I would be great, or that I could achieve anything I put my mind to. He did not speak a blessing over me, as a father should. No, instead, he made me feel as though I was the

'black' sheep of the family since all my other siblings were high coloured and pretty and I was "big, fat and black!" And of course, I believed him.

My father's words further imprisoned my broken soul. They created a cacophony of tears and pain that further ensnared me. In fact, for many years of my life this was the proclamation around which my life would orbit. We all know how important appearance is to a teenager. It is at this time that many fears surface and teenagers, especially girls, are in dire need of a father's acceptance in order to validate them and build their confidence. My dad had failed miserably.

𝐈 did not look into the mirror much after this declaration. It did not make sense to me to do so because all I saw was the persona my father had declared me to be. The reflection staring back at me was always *"big, fat and black"*; in fact, these words would scream at me whenever I looked into a mirror, even well into adulthood. It was because of this, along with the constantly negative input from my immediate family, friends and other relatives that I stayed over weight for most of my life. Compounded by the experiences which I shared earlier, I was now convinced that an overweight, big, fat, black woman is exactly who I was meant to be. In reality and in retrospect, this was just

another childhood experience that the enemy was seeking to use to entomb me into a life that I was not built for.

Where was the blessing I deserved? Fathers have a powerful role to play in the lives of their children. A common scene from the Old Testament was where the father would gather the children together and bless them as he told them *who* they were. The father's words were a powerful determinant of the type of destiny their children would fulfil. I have recognized that sometimes, fathers speak out of ignorance, or they speak out of their own pain. This is true especially for fathers who are not walking in submission to God or seeking to fulfil His purpose for their lives. These fathers will act out of the flesh and inflict on their children the same type of pain to which they were exposed. I can still recall the stories that my dad told me as he chronicled his own rejection from his parents as well as being the 'black sheep' of his family. His mother for one reason or another preferred his brother above him and her words to him tore him up on the inside. Isn't this scenario familiar? My dad grew up and got married, twice! Yet he carried the same pain of his childhood into his relationships with his own children, even though it had inflicted serious pain on him. His negative childhood experiences were carried over into my

generation simply because they were not dealt with in his own life. He had not submitted his life to God in order to allow this to be changed in his own life. Childhood experiences, especially negative ones that are not effectively dealt with will be carried over to the next generation and this is exactly what the enemy wants because he is not just after us, he is after our *seed*. Negative experiences are a trap that have the potential to permeate more than one generation unless they are recognized and effectively dealt with. The good news is that these negative experiences can also be the catalysts for major changes in our lives. When we recognize them for what they are and that we have the power to change their negative influences by the choices we make about how we view them, they will become defining, watershed moments for us that bring us closer to fulfilling purpose.

"Shut up! Stop that screaming in my ears! I can't take it!

These words were commonplace in my home as I was growing up. Although both of my parents would express their dislike for my singing, it was mainly my dad who complained. Whilst growing up, I wanted nothing more than to be a singer. Whitney Houston was popular then so I am sure there was some measure of screaming on my part. Singing, like writing was another one of my

passionate desires. I met with many challenges in my pursuit of this passion but one of the greatest discouragements for me was the constant berating I got whenever I attempted to sing aloud at home. This continued for numerous years until I was convinced that singing was just not for me. I remember that I literally hated the sound of my own voice at one point. Someone said that most persons do not know what they can do, because they are constantly being told what they cannot do. I definitely fell into this category for a while. Negativity is the type of environment that kills hopes and dreams and fosters *stinking thinking*. Left unchecked, my father's words would have

hindered the growth of my psalmist gifting and the enemy would have won again.

Another principle at work here is the demonstration of the power of a father's words. Your father could either bless you or curse you with his words and you will be bound by them to fulfil them until *you do something to change them.* My father's declaration crushed my soul and when combined with the other negatives in my life, they entrapped me into a persona that was not mine for many years of my life. His words hemmed me in until God, who is my **Real Father**, took me up and brought me through many experiences so that I am who I am today. I am vehemently aware that I

have not yet reached the pinnacle of His plan or purpose for my life but I am also cognizant that I am not where I was when I first started this journey.

CHAPTER FIVE – FEAR

"What is your deepest fear?"

Someone called fear the opposite of faith, I call it the ENEMY of faith! Today, many of us are in bondage because of the spirit of fear! Fear stops us from being who God has called us to be. It goads us to conform when God has called us to stand out. It cripples our ability to walk in the liberty of the Spirit. The Bible says "where the Spirit of the Lord is, there is liberty" (2 Corinthians 3 vs. 17). How many believers do you know, who are actually walking in complete and total freedom? Think about it, as a matter of fact, make a list. How many

did you come up with? What about you, are you on that list?

Fear erodes. It eats away at plans and dreams. It deters you from pursuing new exploits. It hinders you from attempting new things and keeps you trapped in your comfort zone. Fear blinds you. It causes you to become encapsulated into a false reality so that you do not step out in faith.

God has not given us a spirit of fear yet many of us battle this spirit in our daily lives. We find ourselves sceptical about doing something new. I know exactly what I am saying because I spent most of my years living in fear. Fear manifests itself in many different ways but mine was intricately tied

up in my ever present desire to please others. A significant part of the emotional challenges I faced growing up was an avid effort to manipulate my feelings of acceptance. Acceptance was not freely offered to me, rather it was usually based on whether or not I had successfully performed a given task. Whenever in my parents eyes I had failed or had not performed as expected, love and acceptance were often withdrawn from me as my punishment. Sometimes it went on for a few days and I would feel compelled to try to *'get into their good books again'* by doing something that they condoned. These types of actions are manipulative in intent and set a very

dangerous precedent for any one, especially for a young woman. This pattern of behaviour was very detrimental to me because I ended up in relationships where this very same pattern was the norm. I was caught in a vicious web where in order to feel good about myself I had to be pleasing someone or even helping others out with their own problems. I pursued and developed these kind of one-sided parasitic relationships for many years, until God Himself, pulled me into His inner circle and retrained me for the type of life that He had created me to live.

Interestingly enough though, it was not only a fear of failure that held me captive for many years of my life, rather, it was the abject fear of success. My thwarted mind-set and belief system made me more afraid to succeed than it did of failing. Failure was expected, because after all, I believed that I was average, but success meant that I had to step out of my comfort zone and try to maintain the façade of success in everyone else's eyes. It meant an avid attempt to live up to other's expectations and the cycle of doing so over the years had already convinced me that this was not at all possible. So, I feared this thing called *success*. As a matter of fact, it crippled me! This fear convinced me to live below the level of my true abilities for many years. I did not now

possess this ability to write. Writing is a latent ability that I held inside because I did not think that I could write anything that could measure up to what others had done. However, God had other plans for me and the vivid childhood memory shown below was used to convince me of that.

"Lynn, stop writing on that wall now!" My mum shouted in frustration. "Have I not told you this before." I shuddered because I knew what was coming next. "Do (whax!), not (pax!), write (palax!) on this house!" she shrieked. I knew that I had once again pushed her to this point. "Cheez," I thought to myself, "why does she not understand that I like to write?"

This was another commonplace scenario in my life as a very young child. I had to write, I loved it! It did not matter how much trouble I got into with my mum, and trust me I got into lots! The punishment I received did not matter and it just did nothing to deter me. Something compelled me to write and write I did. I wrote on the chairs, on the table, on the walls, on books, books of all kinds, my books, my sister's books, my dad's books, my mum's books. Once there was space to write and I could find a pen, pencil, crayon or a piece of chalk, I wrote. I just could not help myself, there was a certain feeling that I got when I wrote, and I loved it! For days, months and

eventually years I wrote on everything in sight and got into trouble for writing on those things on which I was not allowed to write until my mum came to a decision.

"You see this wall here?" she said one morning. "This is your wall. You can write all that you like, with whatever you like. You can draw, colour, do whatever you want but do not, I repeat, do not write on my furniture or my books anymore! Do you understand me Lynn Alleyne?" "Yes mummy," I gleefully responded.

There it was, another victory for me. I could write whenever I wanted to, whatever I wanted to on this wall because this was my space to create. "Yes!" I thought, enamoured by the possibilities that lay ahead of me. It was on this space that I wrote until I went to school and learned about the proper place to write. At this point my mother simply painted the wall.

Your question must be, what happened to this raging passion over the years? Well, like most things we attempt to do in life, if we do not *think* we can do it, or set our minds to achieve it, we never will. I lost my love for writing somewhere along the way, as my beliefs about what I could do changed dramatically. Fear will convince you to live the life of someone that you are not. It will create thought patterns and a belief system that diametrically oppose the truth about who you really are. You will expend energy

trying vehemently to please others around you as opposed to being who you were created to be and living up to your truest potential. That is exactly what played out in my life until my encounters with God caused me to see differently.

CHAPTER SIX – CALLED TO BE DIFFERENT

"Religion Calls for Conformity; Relationship Calls for us to BE!"

One of the most important lessons that I have learnt so far is that our relationship with our heavenly Father is the single most important relationship that we will ever have in this life. Everything else flows, or rather, should flow, out of this connection. The problems that we face in life and how we deal with them are intricately linked to this critical relationship. It is not a fairy-tale relationship where everything is hunky-dory and falls into place seamlessly, but the Father loves us and everything that He does

for, in and through us is motivated by that love. Acceptance of His love is how *stinking thinking* is really changed.

Because of my *stinking thinking*, I did not believe this as I grew up. I could not. Even worst, I did not believe this even after I became a Christian at the age of sixteen. Although I have been serving God for the past twenty odd years, it took me awhile to be utterly convinced of His love and acceptance. Sometimes we go through the motions with God and we equate what we do for Him as evidence that we have accepted His love but it goes much deeper than this. When our lives are fraught with challenges and difficulties, believing that God really loves us is a challenge. I simply could not fathom the type of love and acceptance that is made readily available to us as we give our lives to Christ before developing a closer and more intimate relationship with my Father. Real lasting change and revelation of who I really am only came as that relationship developed and grew. If we want to reverse the thought patterns that we have inherited due to our childhood experiences, we will have to develop the type of relationship with God that frees us to be who we are. It's sort of like learning to lay float on the water. To float successfully, we must let go of fear, totally relax in the water, allow some of the water to go into our ears all the whilst

believing that we won't sink. Achieving this takes a lot of trust but when we have mastered it, the buoyancy of this experience cushions us and causes us to relax in the water as it engulfs us. Just as we freely relax in the water, we must freely relax in our relationship with our heavenly Father.

Religion teaches us to conform and be like someone else but a relationship with the Father calls us into a place of BEING. God wants to bring all of us to this point. He wants us to be the expression of God in the earth. Where we learn to BE exactly who God has called us to BE.

The word of God declares that "…. *the earnest expression of the creature awaits the*

manifestation of the sons of God." (Romans 8:19) God wants us to **manifest** our destiny in the earth but living in fear will stop you from becoming the expression of God in the earth. Unfortunately, many of us choose to remain in bondage to fear and the spirit of religion encourages us to do so.

It is customary for us to have religious experiences where we learn many religious don'ts: do not touch, do not taste, do not talk to, do not associate and such like. We learn the rudiments of being good Christians who will make it to heaven by the things we observe. But, it is our **personal encounters** with God that will be the most significant learning experiences that we will ever have

in our lives. There is a certain measure of uniqueness in those experiences that religious dos and don'ts will never allow us to experience. For instance, the Apostle Paul's encounter with God did not look exactly like that of the other apostles, but he was still an apostle, called by God. In fact, when God called him, he had to be whittled away from the mainstream body of believers until such a time as His training was completed. God, through the Holy Spirit, trained him for approximately three years before releasing him into the mainstream body of believers.

After his Damascus encounter with God, Paul did not go immediately to the other apostles and announce his ministry, he did not consult with man or with those who had a similar calling for their earthly wisdom. No, he went away and separated himself in order to hear from God and develop the type of relationship that would guide him in all his future endeavours. *(See Galatians 1:17)*. This was important because the things that God had for him to do did not look the same as that of the other apostles, neither did they look like what he had been doing previously. His mind had to be reprogrammed and wired the way God wanted, so he had to seek God to find out exactly who he was and what he was called to do. There are many important principles

that we can learn from Paul's actions after his encounter.

Everyone's journey may not necessitate this level of separation from the body of Christ but the principle of seeking God to find out exactly who we are is paramount. We must not be afraid to hear from God for ourselves. We are His people and His sheep and God has assured us that His sheep know His voice. Too many of us are dependent on prophecies and words of knowledge brought by others. Again, nothing is inherently wrong with these either, but the highest principle is that when God has established a relationship with us, He speaks and we must in turn learn to listen. Most of the time we do not hear Him because we are afraid to make a mistake. We are afraid that we will say God said, when He has not said anything, but the only way to change this is by doing. We have to step out in faith and follow the voice of God. To combat this in my own life, I had to come to the realization that God is sovereign and I am human, therefore, if I decide to listen to Him and I make a mistake, He is quite able and equipped to change things and set me on the right path. The important thing is to refuse to live in the fear of making a mistake. It is this fear that really hinders us from pursuing the type of personal relationship that God desires to have with us.

"And I will give them a heart to KNOW me, that I am the Lord: and they shall be my people, and I will be their God: for they shall return unto me with their whole heart." Jeremiah 24:7

"And they shall be my people, and I will be their God:" Jeremiah 32:38

God's real desire is a close, intimate, personal relationship where He speaks and communes with us freely, similar to the relationship which He had with Adam and Eve where He would commune with them in the Garden of Eden. I believe strongly that although the dispensation when God spoke to the people through the priest ended when Christ died and the veil of the temple was torn in two, many of us have unwittingly substituted the 'man of God' for the priest and as a result do not earnestly seek to pursue the Father for ourselves. We become dependent on their sermons and their interpretations of God's word instead of reading His word and listening to the Holy Spirit for ourselves. Again, I must reiterate that there's nothing inherently wrong with listening to sermons, words of knowledge or prophecy because prophets, pastors, teachers and the like, are God's gifts to the Body of Christ to help to bring us to the point of maturity. Ultimately though, God wants to speak and commune with us directly. It is no longer about temples made with hands, as

we are now His temple. He dwells on the inside of us, so we cannot depend only on the external voices of His servants, we must be able to *know* and *trust* the voice of His Holy Spirit who indwells us.

Essentially, spending time in the presence of God is another important part of the process of changing our mind. For, it is in the presence of God that truth is revealed. I believe that this is one of the reasons why Adam and Eve hid in the garden at the sound of the voice of God walking in the garden *(Genesis 3 vs. 18)*. They did not only hide because of their sin but because of the truth that was revealed to them in His presence. Knowing the truth is more than just acquiring head knowledge, it is knowing God because He is the truth. Many of us are in bondage and remain in bondage because we do not know God for ourselves. Remember, it is the God of the religion that we must know and not the religion of God.

CHAPTER SEVEN – THE WORD

"If you don't programme your mind, someone will do it for you"

Allow me to stray away from the norm a bit my friend and share some snippets of wisdom that are sure to set you free. If you truly want to change your mind, you are going to have to develop some courage to go against the norm. Changing your *stinking thinking* will involve more than passivity. It will not be an easy process where we adhere to a simple step-by-step guide and 'voila' we come out on the other side of *stinking thinking*. No, we will have to change the way that we see ourselves by taking action to programme our minds so that we can live the way that God wants us to. One of the ways I did this was to memorize scripture.

As believers, it is really an imperative that we move to a place of maturity where we are no longer 'tossed to and fro by every wind of doctrine'. In other words, we must know where we stand and why we stand there. We must be convinced and not just convicted. Our lives must consist of more than just spouting mere words about the gospel of Christ. God intends for us to be more than just talkers. Too many of us have settled into a place where we can talk the talk but we do not see the importance of living the principles of the word as opposed to just talking about them.

Carriers of the glory of God will not be mere speakers of the Word, they will be doers. The glory of God will be reflected in the things we do and not just the things we say. It will be a lifestyle of glory that will draw others to Him.

Most Christians live their lives from earth to heaven. The renewed mind understands that we live from heaven to earth. *"Thy will be done on earth as it is in heaven". And has seated us together with Christ in heavenly places."* We live in heaven. We are in the world but not of it. No, I cannot fully grasp the import of all of this with my mind, in fact it takes a radical faith to believe it because we see the things on this earth with

our physical eyes. However, the single most empowering and liberating experience for me was my decision to take the word of God *literally*. For almost five years, I read no other religious or inspirational book besides the Bible. I began to learn the Bible verse by verse. I decided to share the verses with friends and acquaintances. This was the beginning of my 'God Daily Ministry' as the 'BB Pastor'. My decision to learn these daily Bible verses showed me that the word of God has answers for all of life's situations and that contrary to popular beliefs it is not irrelevant and antiquated. Rather, it is ALWAYS relevant. If we are open to God's word and its principles, we will find answers

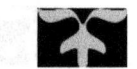

to most of the challenges we face in our lives. The word only becomes irrelevant when we refuse to accept its principles. I have found that we often reject these principles on account of preferring someone else's opinions above and beyond its truths. Or, because we sometimes prefer the humanistic principles that are pushed by many as current truth, but which often times are diametrically opposed to the word of God.

If we want lasting change in our lives, we must also get a handle on our emotions. Anyone who is governed by emotions will have severe difficulty following this prescription and may find his or her life to be similar to riding on a roller coaster. In this roller coaster experience they will experience intense emotions often called mood swings or moodiness. Do not misunderstand me, God has made our emotions and so there is nothing wrong with expressing them. However, it was never His intention for us to be led by our emotions. The word of God clearly says, *'Walk in the Spirit and you shall not fulfill the lust of the flesh'* (Galatians 5 vs. 16). Walking according to the Spirit is a decision. It's an act of the will not an emotional exercise that we do based on how we feel. As real as our emotions are, they will always hinder us from applying Biblical principles and truths to our lives. In fact, because of the sinful nature of man,

emotions are oftentimes diametrically opposed to the truth of God. We will not always feel like doing what God says, therefore, we cannot go through life simply based on emotion. The reality is that this does not always happen, especially with women who are the more emotional creatures. If we are going to walk after the Spirit and not after the flesh, we must in fact submit our emotions to God.

Emotions affect our relationships with others and our faith in God. They may also cause us to develop a number of defence mechanisms to protect ourselves from what we perceive to be potentially dangerous. God is our defence; our protective measures often result in our pushing others away. Simply put, our ungodly beliefs or *stinking thinking* can cripple us and hinder us from achieving our God given potential and purpose in life. Dr. Myles Munroe has said that the graveyard is the richest place on earth. This is an unfortunate fact but surely within the corpses of the deceased lay much of the world's riches as their potential and abilities remained 'unearthed' because they have never dealt with their emotions or *stinking thinking*.

Unchecked and uncontrolled emotions can lead to the setting up of further strongholds in our lives. A stronghold is a mind-set, impregnated with hopelessness

that causes us as believers to accept as unchangeable, something that is contrary to the will of God. *See Luke 11 vs. 21-22.* An ungodly belief is a belief that is contrary to the word and the will of God. These beliefs and strongholds comprise our *stinking thinking* and hinder our spiritual growth. If we are going to change our lives in order to bring alignment with the will and word of God, it is very important that we deal with our belief system.

The word of God has the power to transform old mind-sets, thus, we must allow it to challenge and change our mind-sets and behaviour. How we respond to the word is key to living a life that aligns with the will of God. Until our lives are built on the word of God and its principles, we will find that we can never fully achieve God's best for our lives. Furthermore, positive changes to our lives that are not based on truth will not be lasting changes. As believers, we must grasp the principle that God is tied to His word; it is His bond. God cannot lie because whatever He speaks comes into existence. If He says that a black shirt is a blue shirt, that black shirt, will change colour and become a blue shirt. If He says that an amoeba is a multicellular organism, that amoeba will change formation and become a multicellular organism. That is the power of the word of

God it activates things in our lives. If we understand and grasp this truth, then we will live life on the basis that whatever God has spoken or written in His word about us must bear fruit when it is applied to our lives. The problem lies therefore, not in the power or the truth of the word but in our acceptance and application of His word to our lives. Our first determination must therefore be to chart our lives according to Biblical principles. It is a decision that we must make in order to experience changes in our way of thinking.

It is also important that we understand that God's will and desire is for us to be with Him and to live for Him here on earth. Too many times, we focus on the enemy and the negative things that he is doing in our lives and the lives of those that are around us, so much so that we miss this revelation. God is our Father and He really loves us and wants us to succeed. As passionately as the enemy hates us and desires for us to fail and ultimately renounce God, God's love transcends this with His strong and passionate desire for us to succeed. God and His angels are feverishly at work on our behalf to ensure that we achieve His best and His will for our lives. God has provided the life of His Son, His blood, the Holy Spirit, His angels, His word, His truth, the fruit of the Spirit, the weapons of our warfare, the

word of our testimony, the five-fold ministry and spiritual gifts. All of these are at work on our behalf to ensure success, but instead of accepting these, we are focused on the devil and his demons and their plans of destruction which we have somehow convinced ourselves are more powerful. The word of God says that there are more with us than against us! (2 Chronicles 32 vs. 7) We are not living as victoriously as we should because we are not appropriating all that God has provided for us. There is a popular saying in Christendom that we shouldn't be so heavenly minded that we can do no earthly good. I am convinced that that phrase emanated straight out of the pit of hell! I totally understand that the saint who coined this phrase may have had good intentions but as they also say, the road to hell is paved with good intentions. We are citizens of heaven. The Bible clearly says that we are in the world but not of it. If everything we watch, know and speak about is from an earthly perspective then we are not being more effective, we are seriously imbalanced and are too earthly minded to be any earthly good. We MUST change our minds!

I have personally seen the exacting and life-changing power of the word of God in the lives of people around me as well as in my own life. Just as the rain waters the

earth, so the word of God waters the life of the hearer. Natural rain causes the earth to bring forth and bud, likewise the word of God causes the life of the hearer to bring forth new things and bud. So, if we want fruitful, productive lives, we must build them upon the foundation of the word. We must delve into it and most importantly, apply it, in order to transform our *stinking thinking*.

Grow, mature, shift, transition, become a person of integrity, please! We cannot claim to be a disciple of Christ, yet have no compassion or integrity; these are the hallmarks of Christ. God is married to His word. He holds it in the highest esteem, so high that the word, which existed from the beginning of time became flesh and dwelt among men. Some of us have split personalities when it comes to manifesting the fruit of the Spirit, yet we still insist on calling ourselves Disciples of Christ. We lie, cheat, and say things that we do not mean. We make promises that we have no intention to keep. We lack integrity, yet we expect to be used by God. Most of us do not want to die like a seed and become buried deep in the ground with a solid root system. We prefer to be fickle like some plants whose roots just rest on the soil and are easily moved, susceptible to the wind and every other animal, vice or device that can easily destroy them. As a people, we often prefer broken cisterns that can hold no water because deep

down on the inside we just want life to be easy. We just want the flashy homes, cars and clothing so that we can appear to be well-adjusted, well-known and flourishing. But, the reality is that there is no flourishing without a well-organized root system. The word is our root system. We are not blessed when we listen to the words of those around us. That is not where the blessing lies. The one who does not walk in the counsel of the ungodly, nor stand in the way of sinners, nor sit in the seat of the scornful is the one who will be blessed (Psalms 1 vs. 1). Even more, we will flourish when our real delight, our real passion, our real purpose is to live the word of God!

"But his delight is in the law of the LORD; and in his law doth he meditate day and night. And he shall be like a tree planted by the rivers of water, that bringeth forth his fruit in his season; his leaf also shall not wither; and whatsoever he doeth shall prosper." Psalms 1 vs. 2-3

This is how true lasting change will occur in our lives. When we make the decision to allow the Word of God to be our bond. When our word becomes *living flesh* and people can believe us. That is the manifestation of the sons and daughters of the living God! Their words become flesh.

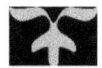

Their yes is yes, it means yes, it has value and their no means no. When they speak, others will not automatically put up their guards because they know that these are people of integrity who will give due diligence to bring to past whatever they have uttered with their mouths. They will live up to their personal expectations of themselves (*that is what our word really is, a personal expectation or commitment that we live out for others to see*). When we do not follow through on our word, we cause the Body of Christ to appear to be weak and sickly with no integrity to deliver what it espouses publicly. We give room for the enemy to make a mockery of Christ all over again.

This is why Jesus could declare that when the enemy comes he will find nothing of himself (Satan, that is) in Him, because Jesus declared His purpose with His mouth and His life manifested His personal expectation of Himself (which was of course based on God's plan for His life). Was it difficult? Of course! This is the reason why He prayed and said if it is at all possible, let this cup pass from me. This is reason why He prayed! We too must pray for the strength and courage to face the obstacles that stand in the way of the fulfilment of our purpose and destiny in the earth. This is the only way to achieve God's plan for our lives. Prayer in the life of the believer is not a spare wheel it is our

steering wheel! It is the way we conquer our adversity. It is the way we survive disappointment and discouragement. It is the way we see the light on our path! We will not change our thinking without the word – God's word or ours and we definitely will not remain firmly planted without prayer. There simply is no easy way around it. It is through prayer that we receive the power to implement our intentions, both our own and God's.

I grew up in church, in the generation where I believe that the idea of reaching our purpose and destiny in the earth was first planted. It became a popular teaching. I can still recall the many sermons and services in which believers spent time on their faces before God, crying out to Him. Many prophets, apostles and teachers were brought in from overseas to pray for believers. Many persons received words, which, for various reasons, they have not seen, come to pass up to this day. I have recognized that achieving our purpose and destiny is way deeper than just singing the right worship song or having a great experience in a revival service! God is not a Maggi; He is not a horoscope, palm-reading session, tealeaves or artificial intelligence! There is no magic portion for reaching our purpose or destiny. Nothing is wrong with the worship song or the experience, they are

necessary parts of our path but too many of us think that these experiences are the end-result and we stay there, stuck, waiting for the words that we heard to magically come to pass. We do not realize that maturity, purpose and destiny are part of a pruning process, they themselves are not the main event. God requires more. He is after us. He wants our obedience, commitment, character, integrity and our heart. This does not happen in one event. It happens when we adjust our thinking and accept His word as truth so that we hold it in higher esteem than anything else in our lives. It happens when we furrow our brows and put on blinders to everything else around us and just take Him at His word! By no means do I suggest not listening to the wisdom of others, there must always be room in our lives for that but my experiences have also taught me that reaching His purpose and achieving His plan is dependent on His Spirit. Not the strength of others, not the power that others hold, it is done by His Spirit. This level of living calls for a deeper relationship with Christ, a passion, purpose and commitment that supersedes every one and every experience that we have ever had in our lives. Applying the word, living the word and prayer are essential parts of this process of change.

CHAPTER EIGHT – OVERCOMING ADVERSITY

"It's not what you see, it's what you believe."

Has God said? Have you heard God but doubt it was really Him because your current reality seems so far removed from what He's called you into? Have you ever been prophesied to and that prophecy is a confirmation of what God has been saying to you but it just seems like it will never come to be? Moreover, as a result, doubt has stepped in because the thing that you are passionate about seems to always evade you. Have you become frustrated and almost believe that the things you dreamt about are just impossible to achieve? Well, let me encourage you. I know for sure that I am a living testimony because right now you are reading from the pages of what was prophesied to me well over sixteen years ago. I went through some phases with this dream. First, I had to overcome self-doubt because I felt that I could not write anything that would hold people's interest. Then I had to overcome fear, then hopelessness because the amount of financial and spiritual challenges that I faced seemingly dictated that I would never be able to achieve what God had spoken to me. Along my journey I also experienced great frustration because every time and I mean every time, I came close to seeing a breakthrough, someone

moved the finish line and I had to go back to having faith and believing that what God promised was true, and that it will come to pass because He said it!

Sometimes the opposition that you will face is so fierce that you are lulled into a false sense of reality and you *settle* into what God only meant for you to pass through. Unless our minds are changed, we will remain there. But my friend let me assure you that overcoming the challenges that you face is possible. To overcome, we must be more convinced about what God has said than we are about what our circumstances seem to say. At times, these circumstances can be so expertly packaged that they can be very convincing; still we must choose to believe what God has said. I am referring both to His logos (written) as well as His rhema (a specific word for a time or season).

Until your thinking about who you are is transformed, you will continue to believe that you are ordinary. You will live like you are ordinary, you will behave as though you are ordinary, you will hang out with those who are ordinary and this type of existence will become your reality. To be released into God's greatest desire for you your mind will need to be changed. The problem is that many of us are waiting on our circumstances to change so that we can be convinced that God is real and that He really loves us.

Many of us believe that if He turns the circumstances around then we will have proof and enough faith to endure. I want to suggest to you that the changing of the mind has very little to do with a turnaround in our circumstances. In fact, I can testify to you that whenever we are going deeper into our relationship with God and when we think that things are about to get better, they can instead become infinitely worst. The enemy will do everything in his might to make you think that God is not with you or that He is not working on your behalf and he will construct the circumstances needed to purvey his MESS-age.

Last year God instructed me to go on a twenty-one day fast. The inner peace and confidence that He had indeed spoken, confirmed that I was walking in obedience with this decision. It was during the summer months. I was very excited because there were somethings that I needed God to change in my life and I believed with all my might that they would be changed by the end of these twenty-one days. The fast went well. I fasted from six o' clock one day until six o' clock the following evening for each of the twenty-one days, having one meal at the end of each day's fast. I spent most of each day before God, listening, writing, praying and believing. I listened to many teachings

by Bill Johnson and a few sermons by Bishop T. D. Jakes.

About twelve days into the fast, my eldest daughter Tia-Lin, my niece Deborah and I were doing Zumba in the family room when suddenly Tia-Lin fell to the ground grimacing in pain and holding her knee. We were in shock for a bit when this happened because she had not made any sudden moves or done anything out of the ordinary. In fact, I am convinced that she was not even moving at this point, but it was as though some evil presence just entered the room and struck her on the knee. My niece and I calmed her down and proceeded to ice her knee. Subsequent medical attention to the then very swollen knee indicated that a tiny piece of bone shard had broken off and she would require a surgery to fix the knee, to the tune of about twelve to fifteen thousand Barbados dollars. I had no money. So it was simple either I would have faith in God or I would spend the rest of my fast worrying about how I was going to pay for this operation. I decided to proceed in faith in spite of the contrary advice I received from one pastor and his wife and even my husband. They were concerned that I was not being practical in my decision.

One Sunday, whilst in prayer and worship with the children, Deborah and I decided that we would anoint Tia-Lin's knee

and pray a prayer of faith because it was all that we had. This incident was significant for two reasons, one, it occurred approximately two days after Tia-Lin had received a prophecy, which confirmed that she was going to dance for God and two, it was on the exact day that I asked my sister in Christ, Minister Destiny from Montserrat, to spend some time with my daughter developing this very same God-given gift. The enemy's intent was clear, he intended to steal, kill and destroy that gift but today, I can testify that she is dancing again and has even had the opportunity to minister to hundreds of youth with a dance which she self- choreographed. She is also currently enrolled in a dance school with a very skilled and Spirit-filled teacher as she continues to hone her gift.

I wish that I could say that this was all that happened, but no that is not how the enemy operates. Before this very eventful twenty-one day fast had ended, my husband also lost a very lucrative contract for our family business because he was provoked to anger by another employee. Remember, this is the fast that I was excited to embark on because I was convinced that it would break some things in my life. Instead, it became apparent that all hell had broken loose on my life. Since this fast, I have endured some of the most intense spiritual warfare that I have

ever experienced in my walk with Christ. I almost lost my home, I was broke; I experienced lack and suffered serious attacks in my family life. In essence, things got infinitely worst instead of better although my heart was in the right place and I was doing what I believed that God had asked me to do.

There is no real formula that I can prescribe for you to overcome your current adversity. There is no step-by-step list of dos and don'ts that I can outline to you. You must apply some of the principles that I have mentioned and you must seek God for yourself. Of course, depending on its origin there will be practical steps that you can take to change somethings. For example, if you've been overspending, spend less; if you're overweight, eat better foods, exercise and the like. But understand this, there will always, always, always be adversity if you are a child of God. He has never promised anything different. Satan is our enemy all of the time, he does not take vacation or long leave, he is always seeking to devour.

We will overcome adversity when our ideas about what is fair or unfair or just and unjust have changed. When we reach the point in our lives where irrespective of the challenges we decide to pray, we choose to worship, we endeavour to give out of our need, we continue to serve God and others

even when everything says *'just give up'*. This is the practical demonstration of our faith. A true son or daughter of God will live by faith in spite of the circumstances that surround them, they will be confident that no matter how the enemy rages and how things change, God will deliver them. Adversity is not the true determinant in our given situations, our faith is. Faith is the currency of heaven, it is how we buy things without money; it is what is most pleasing to God. He is moved to act on our behalf when He sees our faith. Faith allows us to sit above our circumstances and to live in spite of adversity.

Jabez prayed and it released him into his greatness because he decided that he would not give up or just accept his circumstances. It was clear that his mind was made up and that it had been changed. Jabez refused to live within the confines of the parameters set by his parents and his circumstances. His was a demonstration of great faith and trust in God. You simply do not pray like this when you are only seeing your childhood experiences and your current circumstances as true. You pray like Jabez when you have received a glimpse of greater possibilities with God; when you have a whole new way of thinking in spite of what you see. There is no record of Jabez's age

when he prayed and asked God to enlarge his coasts and that he might not cause pain, so we do not know how long his transformation took, or how long it took for him to change his *stinking thinking*. What we do know is that it is possible. Do not set up a permanent place of abode in what were only meant to be temporary circumstances.

CHAPTER NINE - EMBRACING THE NEW!

"Character is not reflected in the things you say; it's expressed by the things you do!"

I am Ambassador Lynn Morgan. I have been a servant of God, worshipper and warrior in the kingdom for the past twenty-four years. I am a pioneer. I am an establisher of the new. Everything I stated before is based on what God has said and shown me over the past few years of renewal. God has caused me to see and experience the NEW in such a way that I am now dubbing myself as an ambassador of the new. God has caused me to walk in a new place, an unchartered, uncomfortable, liberating,

transformational place! I have no forerunners that I personally know but I know that I am not the only one in this place. Each night for the past three years, the Holy Spirit would awaken me and prepare, re-train, direct and empower me for this new walk. My message therefore, is not for everyone. It is one not just for the **'called'** it is for the **'chosen'**! When we get rid of *stinking thinking*, it frees us to see, know and be exactly who we are created to be. We will boldly declare who we are to the world not out of arrogance but out of the quiet confidence of the relationship, which we have developed with our Father.

In the kingdom of God, albeit in the army of God it is imperative that you know who you are and who you are called to be. You must know your season, calling, purpose, time and even more importantly, you must KNOW your God.

And such as do wickedly against the covenant shall he corrupt by flatteries: but the people that do KNOW their God shall BE STRONG, and DO exploits. Daniel 11:32

A close examination of this verse will cause us to recognize that *knowing* comes before *being* and *being* comes before *doing*. It is evident that in all our future exploits,

doing will come from, emanate from and emerge from *being*. Gone are the days when the people of God charismatically preach a message that we have not yet experienced. We will preach with our lives! Our enemy knows that our strongest **being** moment will produce a ***doing*** moment, thus, we experience some of our strongest attacks at the moment that our faith is strongest. The process is simple really. **You must BE who you are before anybody knows who you are.**

Oftentimes we say God is doing a new thing but in actuality, we are really expecting it to fall within our preconceived parameters. We say that we are embracing the new but we expect it to look like what happened at Grace & Truth Assembly (not a real church) last year when we visited their revival. Or, we are expecting to feel like Sister Sara (not a real person) described in last week's prayer meeting. We usually have a picture in our minds of what this new thing that God is doing or about to do, should look like. But here's the real shift, when God does something new it does not look like the old! That's why He said, it's created in the now (new) not long ago, so we can't say we've heard it before.

When God is ready to reveal another dimension of that which was previously hidden and unknown to us, He will create

some new things. Yes, I said CREATE! The word says it! God is finished with CREATION but He is not finished with CREATING. Some of us think that God rested on the seventh day and that He is still doing just that, sitting on the throne. Let me destroy some more theology here. God does not just sit on His throne doing nothing, receiving prayers and moving us like pawns, He is still busy working and creating. If you think that my text is from the Old Testament and therefore not relevant, let's read:

But Jesus answered them, My Father worketh hitherto and I work. John 5 vs. 17

Then Jesus answered and said unto them, verily, verily, I say unto you, the Son can do nothing of himself, but what he seeth the Father do: for what things soever he doeth, these also doeth the son likewise.
John 5 vs.19

Just ponder on these truths for a bit. If we are going to be exactly who God has called us to be we must shift our old way of thinking and embrace the new thing that He has called us to be.

A major shift in my life has taken place recently and the evidence of this shift is a new look. I remember God distinctly saying

to me that I will be unrecognizable to others but distinctly and undeniably His. It was more than just weight loss, it was really a system reboot, a reprogramming of old mind sets and old ways of thinking that had previously sabotaged me. These beliefs had made me a quitter because of embarrassment and the belief *(stinking thinking)* that I could not accomplish things that required physical strength or ability. Do you remember that childhood memory from church sports? That was when this seed was planted and with no environment to deal directly with that seed, that little incident produced thought patterns that really and truly if God had not stepped in when He did, would have led to an early and untimely death on my part. I was heading down a path that was not conducive to longevity.

I was a quitter when it came to anything physical simply because I was self-conscious and held misconstrued patterns of belief that were based on unfortunate childhood experiences. I was not a quitter in all areas though, but I certainly had the misbelief that the only things I could perform well in were the things that required mental ability or intellect. Yes, my beliefs about what I could achieve had changed since childhood and I accomplished many things that I had not previously believed that I could. I got all of my

educational degrees with honours and distinction and I began to sing and to write songs. I was no longer shy and reserved but had become emboldened and, I was a leader in many different spheres of my life. These achievements could convey that I had already conquered many of the negative experiences of my childhood. Spiritually my faith grew but physically I was weak and a quitter. Isn't this the common stance of many of us believers though? We are stalwarts in faith but when it comes to practical things, we lack the drive, integrity and character to face the vicissitudes of life? I have found that it is the practical that really matters. It is what we actually *do* that

displays the power of God that is at work in our lives. That is why Peter could say *'but such as I have give I thee'* (Acts 3 vs. 6); we can only give out of the substance that we have.

My weight loss journey is an acknowledgement of the fact that I have come to recognize the importance of applying my belief in God to all areas of my life. This is to be the lifestyle of a true disciple. It is not what they say, but what they do that demonstrates their lifestyle and beliefs to others. I recognized that I am more than just 'someone who lost weight', rather, I am someone who has done a 180° turn in their belief system and whose 'new' belief system pushes them to accomplish

major hurdles in the spiritual, emotional, intellectual and physical arena.

"I have been called to display the glory of God!"

I have said it before, you have probably said it as well. This is a common and almost cliché saying amongst kingdom citizens. I have come to recognize that God's glory is not sectioned off at our will and fancy. It cannot be partitioned. The way that the glory operates is that it must be manifested for others to see in every single area of our lives. This is how the world and the devil will know that we have traded our *stinking thinking* for new paradigms. This is what will minister to our family members and

work colleagues. We will be the Bible that they read as the WORD in us becomes flesh and dwells among men!

"Changed mind = Changed life!"

CHAPTER TEN – GUILT

"There is therefore now no condemnation!"

The placement of this chapter may seem somewhat strange to you. You may wonder, for example, why after talking about the new would she go back to talk about guilt, especially after having dealt with fear in an earlier chapter. Well, that's how important and significant dealing with guilt and its effect is. I'm sure you've felt it before. In fact, guilt is one of the most potent weapons used by the enemy to keep us in bondage in our thinking.

The effect of guilt is similar to that of fear. It will cripple you and cause you to commit yourself to things that you are not even called to do simply because you have a great or burning desire to fit in. Many Christians are kept in bondage because selfish and corrupt leaders use the word of God to beat them into subjection and fill them with a sense of duty and responsibility that is not theirs to carry. I have experienced this abuse first-hand, having been a servant leader in an assembly for exactly eight years and also being aware of many Christians who are torn about their sense of duty and responsibility to their family, home, Church and God. Until you have settled this battle in your mind, you will not experience the complete freedom

that accompanies total acceptance of who you are, by God. The emotional burden of guilt that many believers carry is simply not of God! It is due to the doctrines of vain, selfish, manipulative men (and women) who have placed heavy burdens on people that they themselves cannot and do not even intend to meet.

To change your *stinking thinking* it is imperative that you deal effectively with guilt in order to go through the process of changing your mind. Have you ever done something that you did not really want to do because everyone else was doing it? For instance, you lacked the necessary resources and you simply could not afford it either financially or time-wise or you had some other pressing things to do, projects that really needed your attention? Your mind screamed no. Your situation screamed no. Common sense said, do not do it now because you have other responsibilities to fulfil. Yet you were convinced that the pastor had heard from God so you decided to go along with it because the entire congregation was going to do it and it was presented expertly as the *'thing that God was calling the church to do'*. You yourself had not heard from God personally but out of *obedience* you decided that you had to do it and just went ahead with it reluctantly. That my friend is how guilt operates. It

goads you and compels you to follow the majority. It will make you give more than you can afford to, attend events that have no real purpose other than to build the reputation of the pastor or to promote a local assembly in the eyes of others. You will participate in activities that have nothing to do with the great commission or the extension of the kingdom of God. You will help build personal kingdoms because of the manipulation and control used by these vipers. You will ignore the fact that there is no scriptural reference to support many of the decisions that affect the entire congregation. In fact, sometimes you are keenly aware that what they require goes

directly against scripture but you give in and you compromise your standards just to fit in. You ignore that small nagging voice in your mind although that voice makes sense, because you believe that it is not possible for you to deviate from the norm and still be accepted. This need for acceptance and to not be seen as the 'rebel' has caused many of us to surrender to a spirit of guilt and its accompanying manipulation and control of our lives.

To overcome this spirit of guilt, you will need to be extremely sure of who you are and of exactly what God has said about you. You will need to know when to say no and to whom you should say no. If you lack

direction in life, a spirit of guilt will always easily manipulate you. God totally accepts us just as we are. He has assigned to each of us a purpose and a destiny and we must not be so afraid to live it out that we allow ourselves to be continually manipulated and guided away from God's intended best for us.

Of course everything must happen within reason, we must also know when God has called us to be a part of something bigger than ourselves and we should serve with all our might when He has done so. When we have developed the type of relationship with the Holy Spirit that allows us to know beyond a shadow of a doubt what our purpose is and what we are called to do, we

will develop the courage to be exactly that person without compromise. You will be better able to prioritize your time and to commit yourself only to what is needful at a given time. Has anyone ever told you that there is a difference between a good thing and a God-thing? Then, dealing with guilt effectively is how you will be able to tell the difference. You are no threat to the enemy when you are sailing along the river of life like a ship without a rudder. His greatest asset is those persons who have eyes but do not see and ears but do not hear what God is saying or doing. However, the moment that you get a real whiff of who you are and why you were created, it's at that exact moment

that you become his greatest threat. When your *stinking thinking* is changed in this area and you have fully embraced the new you. It's then that you will be set free from guilt and you will set many others free as well.

CHAPTER ELEVEN- GIVE UP? NEVER!

"Hope Against All Odds!"

"Hope against all Odds, No matter what you're going through,

You will realize your dreams, If you believe in what God said to You,….."

When I penned the words to this song, I remember sitting forlornly in my classroom, engulfed by pain because of something that had happened between my husband and myself. The words and tune flowed as easily as the tears that streamed down my face, not just because of my pain,

but because I was overwhelmed by the promise of God. It has been over eleven years since I wrote those lyrics. I have had the opportunity to share the song **_Hope Against All Odds_** with many persons locally, regionally and internationally on numerous ministry expeditions. It has ministered tremendously to most of them. However, I finally came to the understanding that the song was birthed to save me. It is God's promise to me in spite of all that I see going on around me. It is the one song that I run to whenever life gets too difficult and the pain of my circumstances seems to outweigh the promise of my Father.

I've known adversity, disappointment and pain. Even as I am writing this book I am still facing some of the most difficult challenges in my life but if I have learnt one thing from all the experiences that I have shared with you, it is to **"never give up!"**

Discouragement, fear, doubt and hopelessness are some of Satan's most potent weapons. It is how he gets into our minds and psyche and seeks to hold us back from ever achieving our goals and reaching our purpose and destiny in life. He often seeks to provide a *mirage* that redefines our reality to one that is not based on God's truth. We have many examples of faith in the word of God and even more, our own

experiences today provide living proof that God will honour our faith in Him. He has never promised us that our lives would be easy but He has promised that He will never leave us. Although it may sometimes feel like He's not there; He never leaves.

I believe strongly that there are many pioneers out there, who are like me to some extent. God has been raising you up in obscurity until such a time as He sees fit for you to be revealed. You are being raised in hardships that are beyond what you could fathom with the natural mind. Sometimes you just do not understand why life is so difficult. You wonder why you have been accused, rejected, overlooked and downplayed for so long. I advance to you that it is largely because of the destiny that is on the inside of you. Our enemy knows the potential, abilities and anointing that God has for you and upon you and he has been consorting and planning to steal your destiny away from you since the time of your birth. You are still here today because God has had you in a *'Moses basket'* throughout your experiences. What you thought was isolation and punishment was God's way of protecting and preserving you for the task that lies ahead. Do not give up. Do not shrink away into the shadows. Rise up and shine for the world to see that you are a carrier of the glory of God.

"You need a delimiter! Most people operate at level 2-3, you are at 6-7, so you need to stay in an environment where you can learn how to operate at level 2-3."

One well-meaning, Holy Spirit filled 'brother' said this to me one day. I do not think I can convey to you the knee-jerk emotional reaction that this declaration stirred up within me. The mere mention of the word *'delimiter'* greatly disturbed me. In fact, I responded as I usually do when I strongly oppose something that I perceive to be in direct opposition to the truth of what God has said. I shouted aloud, *"that Devil IS a liar!"* An experience like this is commonplace anytime you desire to move to a new place in God. In case you are wondering exactly what a delimiter is, let me explain. A speed delimiter as it is correctly called is a device that limits the top speed of a vehicle. It is a method of on board speed restriction! Unbelievable! But, this is typical of the enemy and his operations. Negative experiences are meant to delimit us by providing the on board speed restrictions that hinder us from being all that we can be, from on the inside.

Whenever we are actively pursuing God's will for our lives there will always be someone who will give you what I like to call *'an opposite word'*. This type of word when

acknowledged and imbibed, will simply serve to delimit you and cause you to operate at a level that does not offend the majority of persons who are around you. Offend them my friend! If you are to be exceptional, you must exceed the normal and aim to be extraordinary. Do not settle! I haven't and I will not, not ever again!

My advisor was right to an extent though, because most believers stay at level 2-3 all of their lives, but God is not there. He is at level 6-7 if we continue with this vehicle analogy, or if we dump it (I prefer to dump it), we will recognize that God is limitless. His way of thinking far exceeds ours. He is way out in the deep! We must go way past the expectations and limitations of others and even of ourselves, if we are to achieve His will, plan and purpose for our lives. We will be forced to make the choice whether to stay with the majority of the people or to push past and delve into the deep. The enemy will go to any lengths to kill our destiny even if it means using a well-meaning brother or sister in Christ with an *'opposite word'*. I listened to that brother respectfully then I respectfully declined to receive that word into my spirit because it was contrary to all that the Father had spoken to me in our times of fellowship.

Time is a key principle when we are in the pursuit of God's plan and will for our

lives. For most of us, we want our revelation of purpose and destiny and the fulfilment of that said revelation to be synonymous and even simultaneous events, but in actuality God alone holds the timetable to our times and seasons. Of course, the choices, which we make when He speaks, are paramount to this process. Nevertheless, more importantly we must acknowledge that change and turnaround do not ultimately lie within us. There must be submission to the divine will of our Father. Although Jesus knew His purpose on earth, He was able to tell the evil spirits not to reveal His real identity for His time had not yet come. The demons even begged Him not to torment them before their time. Jesus understood the importance and significance of timing and so does the enemy and his cohorts, we must too. Modern religion teaches us that we hold all the power to change our circumstances within us. In fact, in a book with a title such as this one, the power to change my mind would lie totally within me. I do not ascribe to this belief totally. We do have power, the power of choice. That has ever existed and will never change. It takes an act of the will to submit to God and to wait on His perfect timing for our lives. However, it is God's timing that eclipses all else.

I recall an experience that led to a deeper understanding of this fact for me. I

felt led to take a different route to work one morning and the lesson that God taught me was so significant I was forced to record it in one of my journals. On that particular morning I just felt a leading in my spirit to change my route to work. But much to my chagrin, as I travelled along this route nothing significant happened. In fact, I had to drive even more slowly than usual as I was stuck driving behind a tractor that was transporting sugar cane to a nearby plantation. As I was about to consider whether or not I had really heard God and conclude that this may not have been the exact route that He wanted me to take, God spoke to my spirit about this experience. He said that this is what the road to obedience and faith looks like. The just SHALL live by faith. God showed me that our faith walk is similar to my driving behind the tractor. I could not overtake the driver because the road on which I was driving was a fairly busy one at that time of the morning and it was fraught with quite a few bends (blind corners) which skewed my view of the road ahead. God told me that just as I had followed His instruction to change my route that morning but could not see the road ahead and therefore had to follow slowly behind the tractor until I could see what was ahead of me clearly; this is exactly how the walk of faith operates. If I had been able to

see what was ahead on this road, I would have taken the normal route but instead I had chosen to follow His instruction. Similarly, the road travelled would require that I move at His pace as I patiently awaited His next instruction. God does not reveal the big plan, or our final destination immediately. The road to obedience and faith is one, which is taken moment-by-moment, totally dependent on Him for the next instruction as He guides by His Spirit to fulfil His call and His will in our lives.

CHAPTER TWELVE – MY TURNING POINT

"A changed life is the evidence that you have changed your mind."

When your mind is changed, you will know it. You will act differently and say things that others cannot understand. Sometimes your actions will cause them to question you and your relationship with God but you will know who you are and why you are here. You will be confident and God assured. One anonymously written quote says that when you know who you are meant to be on this earth, you will *never ever* want to be anyone else.

Changing my *stinking thinking* was really a process and a willingness to continuously submit to the Holy Spirit. There was a lot of pushing and pulling as the gradual changes took place and I only became clued in to exactly what God was doing close to the end. I recall that when I first started questioning the status quo and way of doing things as a Christian, I was eighteen years old at the time and it was as though God suddenly lifted the veil off my eyes and I was seeing everyone for who they really were. This rocked my world. I did not know how to proceed because it felt as though all the spiritual giants I had set up in my mind had suddenly fallen and all that remained were the broken, fallen, fragile men and women. At this stage, I just did not know where to go next. I remember running to God for answers. I think maybe the process began then. Unfortunately, it was abruptly aborted because many in religious circles are quick to shoot down any teenager who dares to question or to test the status quo. One of my very dear and respected pastors saw the change in me and said he could not wait to see me on fire for God as I had been before. This set off a chain of guilt and further questioning as I sought God to find out where I had gone wrong and lost my fire. There's much more to that story but I felt the need to mention it because I know

that it was when I had begun to think for myself and ask questions of what I was seeing and the standards that others had set as 'God's standards'. It took many more years and more mistakes to propel this process along.

One thing is certain though, to move from where you are now you will have to overcome fear and doubt and you will need to go against the status quo. God's word, His presence and His will must become the most important things in your life. You must purpose like those three, well four, Hebrew boys that you will not be contaminated by the world and its standards.

It will take determination and zeal for God to make it to the end of this journey.

Based on my experiences, it is my belief that when your mind is changed, God, through His Holy Spirit will give you the list of practical things and steps that you need to take in order to walk on the path that He has chartered for you. My list will not resemble yours because your circumstances may be unique and may require another mode of attack in order for you to rise above them. When I got the call from God to go against the status quo of the day, I had to test it to ensure that I had heard correctly. I actually asked God, "how can this be you, isn't the Church yours?" To ensure that I was not

going against His will, I tested the call with my family members at the time, my husband and eldest daughter and none of them were opposed to what God was saying. This proved to me that God had already prepared the way for what He had asked me to do. This has been one of the most uncomfortable parts of my journey but I know it is the most powerful and it is exactly what I need in order to be fully prepared for the work that God has for me to do. It is not a place I envisioned for myself. I had grandiose dreams that all involved being an active member of a local Church. Something happened along my journey that catapulted me into this place that I now speak about.

You may read those gory details in my next book, **"Deception: Satan's Deadliest Weapon"** but suffice to say that I had to go through many challenges most of which led to this experience that I am still going through today. I had become accustomed to the norm, church every Sunday and ministry commitments to fulfill and such like but my Father was drawing me away for intimacy and listening, hours and hours of journaling and loneliness beyond my wildest imagination. This has been uncomfortable but now I know I am smack dab in the midst of where my Father wants me to be. This is the most important thing about having a relationship with Christ. If we are going to

effect any change in this world, we must know that we know, that we know what we know beyond any doubt, what God is saying to us. These are not days for doubters or for those who are unsure about who they are in Christ because they will be gobbled up and eaten for lunch by the roaring lion who seeks to steal, kill and destroy our future. This is where knowing who you are and knowing your God come into play. There will be attacks and offenses coming at us left, right and centre but we must not be tossed to and fro by every wind and doctrine. No, we must be of ourselves, convinced that we are doing exactly what God wants, so that even if an angel were to come down and tell us to do differently we would be able to be discerning and know what to do.

We like to think that there is something spectacular that we can do to win God's approval and favour. The reality is that we are all subject to His timing and will. Contrary to many of the teachings that we receive in religious circles we cannot send the Holy Spirit anywhere. No! He sends us. We cannot command the Holy Spirit to perform any task. God has always and will always continue to give us the freedom of choice but I can assure you that He will always respond to our faith. He has no choice because He is bound to His word and His word says that faith is what pleases Him.

In a previous chapter, I used the Apostle Paul's encounter with God to highlight how God communicated with Him in spite of the already established apostles. When God was ready and the time was right, He stopped Paul in His tracks. Paul had been persecuting the church on God's behalf and was convinced that what he was doing was right, until He had an encounter with God that totally shifted his way of thinking. We cannot cajole God into responding but we must ensure that we are in the right place at the right time in order for Him to do what He wants. It is imperative that we cultivate the type of relationship that allows Him to guide and direct at His will. The disciples left everything that they were accustomed to when Jesus gave them the word of invitation. We must aim to live our lives with this type of heart. So that we go where He sends us, when He sends us to do it. We must come to the place where like Jesus we can attest that our meat is to do the will of the Father. Real power lies not just in the mountain experiences when we are prophesied to and promised a better life; it lies in the *humility* we have to do what God says in spite of what we see around us. Jesus demonstrated this when He uttered the words *'nevertheless, not my will'* (Luke 22 vs. 42). This takes humility, it requires will power, it demands determination and it builds our faith.

CHAPTER THIRTEEN – THE CALL

"So what's next?"

By now, you my friend should be charged, empowered and ready, to fight on in this great big battle. I hope by now that you are ready to tell the devil that you have changed your mind!

The longer you stay within the confines of other people's expectations the more you will become like them. This is why it is imperative that you break free from those shackles and find out exactly what are God expectations of you and live up to those instead. The enemy longs for us to look back and to be locked into the mistakes, pain and regret of the past but God is longing to release us into our future, into the things that He has prepared for us. This is why changing our minds is of utmost importance. It is important for us personally as well as for our future generations. Our freedom sets them free to pursue and be all that God has for them to be.

God's plans are dynamic. What He is busy orchestrating in and through your life is needed by someone somewhere else in the world and what He is busy orchestrating in someone's life is necessary in your part of the orchard. If I had never obeyed God's call to come away from the norm, you would not be reading a book written by me on this

particular subject. Our obedience to God is paramount to the process which we go through and to His overall work in the earth. Oftentimes we are told that it is the destiny or the destination that is most important. We rejoice when others have reached the top of their game and are successful according to the world's standards. But, God's ways and standards are very much the opposite. He is very interested and invested in the process that we go through as we are prepared for our predetermined destination. That is why Job could testify that God knows the way that he takes and *"when He has tried me, I shall come forth as gold"* (Job 23 vs. 10). God is with us through every step of our journey even when we are convinced differently. Society and religion have painted a picture of a utopia that we will achieve when we become believers but this is a lie from the pit of hell. The Bible warns us that the world will hate us just as it hated Christ. Offenses must and will come, but the good news is that Christ has overcome the world and all the power and help and authority that we need is freely available to us. The word of our testimony is evidence that we too have overcome. I can attest to the fact that faith fluctuates but the faithfulness of the one in whom we put our faith is unchanging. Thank God that He has said that our faith only has to be the size of a mustard seed in

order for Him to be moved to act on our behalf. There are situations that we face which can be so daunting that they will cause you to doubt that you are doing the right thing by walking in faith. It is at times like these when that mustard seed becomes the easiest target to make. I have lost some friends along the way and their passing has caused me to realize that there is no fairy tale ending to this life we live. The decisions that we make about how we will respond to the life that we have been given will determine the type of ending that takes place here on earth. We must choose to fight in order to change.

Finally, let me encourage you as you go through this process where God is sanctifying you to Himself. Friend, you are not overlooked; you are hidden. God has you temporarily out of sight so that He can develop, strengthen and prepare you. The testing that you faced will bring a testimony that will bless many others and help to set them free. At the correct moment in time, God Himself will cause your breakthrough in a mighty and powerful way.

APPENDIX 1 - SOME PRAYER POINTS

❖ Holy Spirit please reveal to me any old mind-sets or beliefs that I have.

❖ Show me old 'truths' or 'heresies' that I have accepted as truths.

❖ Change my viewpoints about who I am and where I am at in God.

❖ Help me to see myself as you see me God. Help me to accept myself the way you do Holy Spirit.

❖ As I move into a new place, help me not to look back at the old longingly.

❖ Lord, grant me the courage to make the changes that you require of me, irrespective of the negative circumstances and discouragement that I am currently facing.

❖ Lord, I believe that fulfilling my purpose and destiny is the most important thing I will ever do. Give me the strength to pursue them.

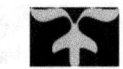

VOTE OF THANKS

The support that I have received from family, friends, acquaintances and even strangers during the writing and publishing of this book has been extremely humbling.

I must mention: Lisa Cummins my friend and sister in Christ who willingly and ably wrote the foreword for my book; Marsha Gay, an educator and dear sister in Christ who sacrificed her vacation time to assist me with editing; Timothy Leach of NiCOMM Solutions, Barbados who willingly offered his services in photography and graphic design; Pastor Felicia Johnson, Prophet Angelow Hickson and Prophet-Teacher Sheldon Miller who along with numerous others reviewed my work; Deborah Ramdin, my niece, fashion consultant, make-up artist, sister in Christ and friend, for all her willing support; my husband Troy and our children who have been stalwart throughout this entire process and of course God my Father!

To everything, there is a season and a time to every purpose under the sun, it is time for this message to be released into earth and God has put everything in place in order to make this happen. The right connections at the right time have resulted in this completed work. To each of you and to my Heavenly Father, I am eternally grateful.

I PRAY THAT THIS BOOK HAS BEEN A BLESSING TO YOU.

FOR MORE INFORMATION ON AMBASSADOR LYNN MORGAN & HER TITLES FEEL FREE TO CONTACT US AT:

Email: ambassodorlynnmorgan@hotmail.com

ABOUT THE AUTHOR

Ambassador Lynn Morgan is an adept event planner, mentor and life coach who loves to write both books and music. Lynn is the composer and main contributor to most of the lyrics heard on the CD God Is Raising Up. She is a prophetic psalmist and is the founder of Open Heaven International, a ministry that focuses on worship, life coaching and mentorship.

Ambassador Lynn Morgan has a passion for teaching and has been an exceptional educator for the past seventeen years. She holds a Bachelor of

Arts Degree in History, with honours from the University of the West Indies Cave Hill Campus, a post-graduate Diploma in Education with distinction in the practice of teaching from Erdiston Teacher's Training College and a Masters in Educational Leadership also with distinction, from the University of the West Indies, Cave Hill Campus.

www.ingramcontent.com/pod-product-compliance
Lightning Source LLC
Chambersburg PA
CBHW060319050426
42449CB00011B/2550